ESSENTIAL 101 TIPS

CACTI &
SUCCULENTS

ESSENTIAL TIPS

101

CACTI & SUCCULENTS

Terry Hewitt

LONDON, NEW YORK, MELBOURNE,
MUNICH AND DELHI

Editor Bella Pringle
Art Editor Gill Della Casa
Managing Editor Gillian Roberts
Category Publisher Mary-Clare Jerram
DTP Designer Sonia Charbonnier
Production Controller Luca Frassinetti
US Editor Laaren Brown

First American Edition, 1996
This paperback edition published in the United States in 2004
by DK Publishing, Inc.
375 Hudson Street, New York, NY 10014
Penguin Group (US)

A catalog record is available from the Library of Congress

ISBN 0–7566–0613–6

Color reproduced in Singapore by Colourscan
Printed in China by WKT

Discover more at
www.dk.com

ESSENTIAL TIPS

PAGES 27-29

WATERING

PAGES 30-31

FEEDING

PAGES 32-38

LIGHT

PAGES 39-43

TEMPERATURE

PAGES 44-49

MAINTENANCE

CACTI & SUCCULENT KNOW-HOW

1 WHAT ARE CACTI & SUCCULENT PLANTS?

The cacti family belongs to a larger group of plants known as succulents. All succulents have specialized anatomy that enables them to survive drought or lack of light.

Succulents can store moisture in fleshy tissue in their stems, leaves, or roots, and many have developed features to reduce water loss. In adverse conditions, they can cease growing and remain dormant.

CROSS SECTION

Water storage tissue

SIDE VIEW

◁ STEM SUCCULENTS
Plants that store large amounts of watery mucus in round or columnar stems. Water loss is kept to a minimum by the small surface area in proportion to volume. Nearly all cacti are stem succulents.

Spines reduce moisture loss

Tuberous roots store water

Fleshy leaves
store water

Lower leaves help
shade soil and
reduce evaporation

△ LEAF SUCCULENTS
*Species with leaves that vary in
size and form, depending on
water availability. When
water is present the leaves
swell to become thick and
fleshy, but in drought they
shrivel or are shed.*

SIDE VIEW

Fleshy stem
and leaves

CROSS SECTION

2 HOW CACTI DIFFER

Cacti are different from other succulents because they have areoles – padlike buds – from which shoots, spines, and flowers grow. Only species of cacti have areoles, but be careful when using this feature for identification as areoles are not always easy to see.

CLOSE-UP OF AREOLES ON SURFACE

◁ ROOT SUCCULENTS
*These plants store
water underground
in tuberous, or
swollen, roots. This
feature enables these
plants to survive long
periods of drought.
Below soil level,
moisture loss occurs
more slowly and
there is less risk of
damage by fire or
grazing animals.*

3 DO CACTI GROW ONLY IN DESERTS?

Although traditionally associated with arid desert and mountain landscapes, some cacti and other succulents inhabit tropical jungles. There the climate is hot and humid and the plants have to contend with a lack of light rather than the usual lack of water. Some jungle cacti, such as *Epiphyllum*, have flattened stems with a large surface area to absorb maximum light.

JUNGLE & DESERT HABITATS ▽ ▷
The success of cacti and other succulents partly depends on their ability to inhabit inhospitable jungle and desert areas where there is little competition from other plants.

4 DO CACTI & SUCCULENTS NEED LESS CARE?

Many believe that because these plants grow in a hostile landscape they require little or no care when cultivated. It is true they can tolerate some neglect and little water but, if forgotten, they will retreat into dormancy. Healthy plants grow and flower annually.

5 WHEN DO THEY FLOWER?

In arid desert regions, long, dry spells ensure cacti and succulents remain dormant for most of the year. To make up for this, many have developed a short life cycle. Once rain falls, they burst into active growth, producing leaves, flowers, and seeds in less than one month.

◁ DAY-FLOWERING CACTUS
Echinocereus triglochidiatus *produces a mass of bright red flowers that open fully in the summer sun.*

Flowers appear in summer when the plant reaches 4 ft (1.2 m) tall

Petals open up to 10 in (25 cm) across

Huge blooms grow directly from cactus stem

NIGHT-FLOWERING CACTUS
In summer, the flowers of Echinopsis scopulicola *open at dusk and close at dawn. The pale petals help moths locate them at night.*

6 WHERE TO BUY CACTI & SUCCULENTS

A huge variety of cacti and succulents can be cultivated but only a limited choice of species – usually those that are easy to grow – can be bought at garden centers or florists. Visit a cactus nursery or local cactus show if you wish to buy a more unusual variety of plant.

Diseased leaves lack vigor

△ UNHEALTHY SUCCULENT

Mound of well-formed waxy leaves

△ HEALTHY CACTUS

HEALTHY SUCCULENT △

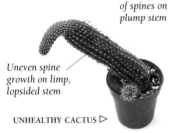

Even growth of spines on plump stem

Uneven spine growth on limp, lopsided stem

UNHEALTHY CACTUS ▷

BUYING HEALTHY PLANTS
When you have decided which variety of cactus or succulent to buy, the next step is to choose a healthy plant. Look for the telltale signs shown here and outlined below.

7 HOW TO SELECT A HEALTHY CACTUS

The stem skin of a cactus reveals a great deal about the plant's health.
• Avoid plants with tired and dull stem skin or ones that have large, unsightly skin blemishes.
• Check that the spines are evenly distributed and are undamaged.
• Look at the soil mix in the pot. If it is fresh and weed-free, the grower has cared for the plant.

8 SELECTING HEALTHY SUCCULENTS

Many succulents are leafy, and by inspecting the leaves you can determine the plant's condition.
• Avoid succulents that have only a few leaves or have pale leaves; this is an obvious sign of poor growth.
• Examine the leaves to make sure that none is deformed.
• Check that the level of soil mix in the pot has not dropped.

9 Easy care for beginners

Many of the species sold by florists and garden centers are ideal for beginners; in fact they have often been selected on the basis that they are easy to care for. These cacti and succulents will tolerate some neglect, and, unlike other species, they produce flowers when only a few years old.

△ PARODIA HERTERI

Pink flowers appear between spring and early autumn

Daisylike flowers appear after two years

FAUCARIA TUBERCULOSA ▷

Triangular leaves tipped with "teeth"

▽ SEMPERVIVUM 'BELLOT'S POURPRE'

EASY-CARE CACTI & SUCCULENTS
CACTI
Cereus aethiops
Ferocactus wislizeni
Gymnocalycium baldianum
Opuntia lindheimeri
Parodia herteri
Stenocactus multicostatus
SUCCULENTS
Adromischus cooperi
Cotyledon undulata
Echeveria elegans
Faucaria tuberculosa
Kalanchoe tomentosa
Sempervivum 'Bellot's Pourpre'
Senecio haworthii

DISPLAY & ARRANGEMENT

10 THE KEY TO A HEALTHY DISPLAY

Cacti and succulents are broadly divisible into desert plants that like dry sun and jungle plants that prefer moist shade. When choosing a selection of plants to grow together, check that they have similar cultural needs, and bear in mind the final location for which they are intended. The more adept you are at matching the plants' needs to the limitations of the site, the more successful your plantings will be in the long run. For example, if you have a sunny spot on a windowsill, select species that thrive in full sun.

FEROCACTUS
HERRERAE

AEONIUM
ARBOREUM

CRASSULA
OVATA

CLEISTOCACTUS STRAUSII
ECHINOPSIS SPACHIANA

INDOOR DESERT DISPLAY

11 HOW LONG WILL THE DISPLAY LAST?

Indoor displays are well suited to the warm, dry conditions of a centrally heated home and will thrive for two to three years. After this, renew the compost and replace oversized plants.

12 HOW TO HANDLE PRICKLY PLANTS

When working with spiny cacti, particularly those with very fine or barbed spines, use thick gloves, a paper collar, or barbecue tongs to prevent your hands from becoming "attached" to the cactus.

PAPER HANDLE METHOD
Fold a length of brown paper into a strip 2 in (5 cm) wide. Wrap the strip around the stem and lift the plant out of its pot.

GLOVED METHOD
Wearing thick gloves, ease the plant out of the pot by supporting the plant in one hand and turning the pot upside down.

13 REMOVING SPINES

Use tweezers to carefully extract cacti spines that become embedded in your skin. To strip out fine bristles that are less visible, pat the affected area with a piece of adhesive tape, or soak in hot soapy water to open the pores.

USING TAPE TO REMOVE BRISTLES

14 SHAPE CONSIDERATIONS

The decorative appeal of cacti lies in their abstract forms, which range from tiny globes to creeping candlelike stems, to huge column shapes. Other succulents also offer a diversity of forms and include shrub- or treelike species or low-lying plants with rosettes of leaves. Some have arching or trailing stems, while others have bulbous forms. In bloom, beautiful flower shapes and colors make an attractive addition to any display of cacti and succulents.

△ LITHOPS
KARASMONTANA

◁ ECHEVERIA
ELEGANS

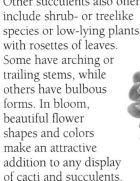

ECHINOPSIS
SPACHIANA ▷

AGAVE
VICTORIA-
REGINAE ▷

CLEISTOCACTUS
STRAUSII ▷

◁ HOYA
CARNOSA × KERRI

ECHINOPSIS
CHAMAECEREUS ▷

△ SENECIO
STAPELIIFORMIS

△ ECHINOPSIS
HYBRID

15 PLANNING THE DESIGN

To create an interesting display, choose plants of similar size in a variety of shapes, textures, and colors. For best results, before planting, try different designs with the plants still in their pots.

EXPERIMENTING WITH DESIGN

△ FEROCACTUS
HERRERAE

16 CACTI & SUCCULENTS IN CONTAINERS

The slow growth and long display life of cacti and succulents make them ideal plants to grow in the limited space of a container. Potted plants can also be moved indoors or outdoors, depending on the weather and which varieties are susceptible to cold, damp, and frost. A very wide choice of pots is available. Select styles and materials that complement your plants, and group containers for maximum effect.

◁ EARTHENWARE JARS
Two columnar cacti in large earthenware jars create a bold but simple display inside or out.

WOVEN
BASKETS △
Plant up plastic-lined baskets with small species that offer a variety of texture.

PAINTED POTS ▷
Brightly painted pots filled with strong-shaped cacti make a striking display.

17 CHOOSING A SUITABLE SITE

Take into account practical points as well as aesthetic considerations before deciding on a site. Ensure that the light, temperature, and humidity conditions suit the plants' needs, and check that the plants will be displayed at a height that shows them off to best advantage.

PLANTS DISPLAYED ON A WINDOWSILL

18 PLANTING IN A RAISED BED

Cacti and succulents can be planted outdoors, but generally only in frost-free areas. Choose soil that is free-draining and a sunny position sheltered from winds. To improve drainage, or when planting in a region with high rainfall, build a raised bed or sloping mound.

1 Clear away any topdressing and dig a hole large enough to take the root ball. Gently tease apart the plant's roots.

2 Position the plant to the same depth as it was in its pot. Fill in and firm the soil. Sprinkle with topdressing.

19 PLANTING IN A WALL CREVICE

Gaps in garden walls filled with shallow soil make attractive sites for establishing succulents that are native to rocky habitats. With the aid of a small tool, such as a spoon, scrape out some of the soil from the wall crevice. Gently insert the plant's roots, and while holding it in place, fill in with new soil mix. Firm the plant in position.

20 TOOLS & EQUIPMENT

Thick gloves, a trowel, and pots are the basic equipment required for planting an indoor or outdoor display. Have a teaspoon handy when filling in a small display with soil mix; there is little space between the plants for a trowel. Remove any dirt or dust from the plants with a soft paintbrush.

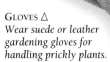

GLOVES △
Wear suede or leather gardening gloves for handling prickly plants.

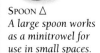

SPOON △
A large spoon works as a minitrowel for use in small spaces.

TROWEL ▷
A wide-blade trowel is ideal for mixing soil mix, digging raised beds, and planting larger containers.

△ BRUSHES
You will need a fine brush for pollinating and a larger brush for removing dirt without damaging plants.

◁ POTS OF VARYING SIZES
As a rule, cacti and succulents grow slowly and produce shallow roots. Both small full-depth pots and shallow pans are ideal.

21 HANGING BASKET DISPLAY

Jungle cacti with arching stems and pendent flowers, and most trailing succulents, are perfect for hanging basket displays. To avoid scorching, place in bright indirect light.

1 Sit the basket in a large pot to steady it. Line the basket with moss and a saucer at the base to catch drips. Fill two-thirds of the basket with soil mix.

CHRISTMAS CACTUS △
Schlumbergera 'Frida', a shade-loving hybrid, produces vivid flowers in winter.

2 Ease each plant out of its pot. Hold the base of the stem in one hand and tease out some of the roots with your fingers, taking care not to damage them.

3 Place three plants in a triangular formation and fill in with soil mix, firming it down with your fingertips. Do not water for 2–3 days to avoid root rot.

22 WINDOW-BOX DISPLAY

The variety of shapes, colors, and textures that distinguish many species of cacti and succulents can be displayed to glorious effect in a window box. Good drainage is key to a long-lasting display that will thrive outside for most of the year. Bring the display indoors in winter to protect from cold.

1 △ Cover drainage holes with shards and a layer of paper to prevent loose soil mix from clogging up the drainage.

2 △ Half fill the window box with soil mix. Take each plant out of its pot and position it so that its rootball is at the same depth as it was in its pot. Fill in with soil mix, pressing gently.

3 △ Brush off any dirt that has fallen onto the leaves. Spoon a layer of gravel over the soil mix to prevent the surface from drying out and stop algal growth.

THE FINISHED DISPLAY
To create this display you need (left to right):
Crassula ovata;
Echeveria elegans;
Cleistocactus strausii;
Aeonium arboreum
'*Atropurpureum*';
Ferocactus herrerae;
Ferocactus latispinus;
Echinopsis spachiana;
Mammillaria bombycina.

— *Place tall plants at the back*

23 PLANTING AN INDOOR BOWL

Small or slow-growing cacti and succulents that favor dry habitats offer enormous scope for creating a low-maintenance desert-style display. Plant in a shallow bowl and position indoors in a brightly lit site, and the display will thrive for two or three years before the plants and soil mix need replacing.

1 △ Mix two parts peat with one part gravel to make a free-draining soil mix. Trowel a layer over the bowl base.

2 △ Decide on a design, placing taller species at the back. Plant each species to the same depth as it was in its own pot. Fill in with soil.

3 △ Once all the plants are in place, lightly firm the surface of the soil mix. Using a fine brush, remove any soil that is lodged between the plants' leaves.

Add pebbles and a topdressing of gravel

INDOOR DISPLAY
For this planting you will need (clockwise from top left): Aeonium haworthii; Opuntia *species;* Echeveria fimbriata; E. elegans; Mammillaria magnimamma. *All those listed above have shallow roots so the bowl need only be 3 in (8 cm) deep. All need very little water and are dormant in winter.*

POT PLANTING

24 WHICH SOIL MIX?

Cacti and succulents will thrive in a potting soil mix that is free-draining yet retains moisture. Special commercial cactus potting mixes are ideal, or you can use a commercial soilless mix with gravel. Alternatively, make your own soilless mix from coconut fiber, peat, bark, and gravel. Soil-based mixes are fine if blended with gravel.

SOILLESS MIX

SOIL-BASED MIX

COMMERCIAL CACTUS POTTING MIX

PEAT

25 HOW MUCH SOIL MIX?

All pot-grown plants need to have their roots covered by soil mix to within ½ in (1 cm) of the rim to enable water and air to reach the roots. In time, soil mix compacts and the level drops so remember to refill it.

WRONG SOIL LEVEL

CORRECT SOIL LEVEL

26 SOIL MIXES

The extent to which the soil drains and retains water, plus its level of acidity, determine which ingredients need to be added and in what quantities.

INDOOR PLANTS

For indoor plants, mix two parts commercial soilless mix with one part gravel. Soil-based mixes are acceptable but can become compacted when dry. A good mix is three parts commercial soil mix to one part washed gravel.

OUTDOOR PLANTS

Assess the quality of the soil before you plant. The majority of cacti and succulents prefer slightly acid soil. To make soil more acid, add peat or garden compost. If the soil is sandy, add one part peat to three of soil. Add gravel to the improved soil.

OUTDOOR CONTAINERS

For outdoor containers and raised beds, make a soilless mix out of three parts of either peat, coconut fiber, or wood bark, and one part small washed gravel; use equal parts of peat and washed gravel to fill pots that do not drain easily.

27 IMPROVING DRAINAGE

Good drainage is necessary to prevent root rot in cacti and succulents. When planting a container, begin by covering each drainage hole with a shard and a layer of clay pellets. Place paper on top to prevent the soil mix from sticking and impeding drainage.

BROWN PAPER LAYER
Place a sheet of brown paper on top of the clay pellets before adding soil. By the time the soil settles, it will have dissolved.

PAPER TOWEL ALTERNATIVE
A layer of paper towels on top of the clay pellets also prevents the new soil from clogging up the drainage system.

28 WHY APPLY A TOPDRESSING ?

Covering the soil with a topdressing of small gravel or crushed stone has many practical benefits. It helps to conserve moisture in the soil, and prevents the surface from drying out. It suppresses weeds and inhibits the growth of algae. It also reduces soil erosion, and prevents splashmarks on the plants during watering. Topdressings must be inert, so do not use limestone, which increases the soil's alkalinity.

GRAVEL TOPDRESSING
A layer of gravel on top of the soil between plants retains the moisture in the soil and ensures a low-maintenance, weed-free bed.

29 WHICH TOPDRESSING ?

As well as serving a practical function (*see left*), topdressings are also decorative. It is best, however, to avoid artificially colored gravels as these detract from the simplicity of the plants.

PEA-SIZED PEBBLES

SMALL GRAVEL

CRUSHED STONE

WATERING

Water only when the meter indicates that the soil is dry

MEASURING THE SOIL MOISTURE

30 KNOWING WHEN TO WATER

Perhaps the most common cause of premature death in cultivated cacti and succulents is overwatering, which rots the roots. Most cacti and succulents can withstand periods of drought, so if you are in any doubt, do not water the plants.

- A moisture meter is the only accurate way to measure how dry or wet the compost is.
- Do not water until the moisture meter indicates almost dry.
- In general, cacti and succulents only need watering when in active growth (usually spring or fall) and need little or no water while dormant (mainly winter months).

31 SURVIVAL WITHOUT WATER

Inappropriate light and temperature are likely to cause permanent physical damage to cacti and succulents but lack of water will not. Cacti deprived of water simply shrink into dormancy as they would in the desert during a drought, and they will quickly revive once watered. When the sun is hot, however, shield plants, or they will suffer scorch damage that is visible as brown patches.

SCORCH-DAMAGED PLANT

32 WATERING CALENDAR

During the year, the water intake of cacti and succulents varies. During periods of active growth, usually spring or summer, they need water every 1–2 weeks, but in dormant periods they survive with little or no water. The plants' seasonal needs are indicated below.

Can with rose is used for outside plants

Increase humidity with a spray-mister

Use small can to water indoor plants

SUMMER
In summer, allow soil or soil mix to dry out almost completely between waterings. It is very important not to overwater in hot weather as most cacti and succulents become dormant. In this state, they are unable to take up water, and if left in wet soil mix, rot from the roots up.

SPRING
In spring, water most plants every 1–2 weeks; indoor plants in small pots need more frequent watering as the soil tends to dry out more quickly. Outdoor plantings, window boxes, and pots, especially those with a topdressing, retain water longer and often need less.

FALL
As in the spring months, fall is a period of active growth, and most plants need watering every 1–2 weeks.

WINTER
In areas where the temperature is above 50°F (10°C), water plants sparingly; in cooler regions, stop watering altogether.

33 WHAT TIME OF DAY TO WATER

The best time of day to water is early in the morning or late afternoon so that the plants have time to absorb the water and any surplus moisture on the leaves or stems before the sun comes out. Watering in full sun can scorch the leaves and eventually kill the plant.

WATER PLANTS OUT OF SUNLIGHT

34 INCREASING HUMIDITY

Most cacti and succulents favor a dry atmosphere, but jungle species thrive in hot, damp environments. To re-create this indoors, or in a sun room or greenhouse, the temperature must be in the range of 70–90°F (21–32°C). Create a high level of moisture in the atmosphere by gently misting the plant's leaves with a hand-held spray. Continue to use a spray mister as part of your watering routine. Like other succulents, these plants can survive drought.

SPRAY-MISTING AN EPIPHYTIC CACTUS

Pour water into the gravel at the base

WATERING FROM THE BASE

35 WATERING METHODS

Water a large collection of plants from overhead with a light spray to prevent soil from becoming dislodged. If you have only a few plants in pots, gently pour water into the gravel topsoil to avoid any splash back. Be careful not to overwater; this can eventually result in root rot.

36 SIGNS OF STEM ROT

Cacti and succulents that are kept in unsuitably cold or damp conditions, or that have poor roots, are prone to rot. Rot fungus penetrates the plant's skin and attacks the tissue, turning it soft and eventually black. If stem rot attacks your potted plants, cut off any healthy stems for cuttings, and destroy the rest. If rot attacks the stems of permanent outdoor plantings, apply copper sulfate.

FEEDING

37 WHY FEED DESERT PLANTS?

In the wild, the sporadic and unbalanced availability of minerals means that desert plants just survive – but in cultivation, with regular feeding, they soon flourish. During the growing season, plants benefit from regular supplies of nitrogen for good top growth, potassium for flowers, and phosphorus for strong root growth.

FLOWERING DESERT PLANTS
Although able to survive in the desert on a low-mineral diet, cultivated cacti will thrive if fed during the growing season.

38 WHEN TO FEED

Cacti and succulents require feeding in two stages. At planting time, mix a base fertilizer into the soil mix. Then apply either liquid or solid fertilizers with routine waterings, but no more than once a week for desert plants or twice weekly for jungle species.

39 WHICH FERTILIZER?

Fertilizers are available from nurseries in powder, granular, liquid, or solid form. They may be organic or inorganic. Organic fertilizers include seaweed; although rich in trace elements, the chemical content of organics is less consistent than inorganic fertilizers.

◁ HOUSE-PLANT TABLES

FERTILIZER STICKS ▽

△ FERTILIZER TABLETS

▽ LIQUID FERTILIZER

△ FERTILIZER GRANULES

FERTILIZER ▷ POWDER

40 SHORT-TERM FEEDING

Cacti and succulents respond well in the short term to tomato liquid fertilizer, diluted to half strength. Do not use this as a long-term solution because its low nitrogen content (only one to five percent of the fertilizer) can cause cacti and succulents to become stunted.

41 SIGNS OF OVERFEEDING

You can tell by the changes in the physical appearance of cacti and succulents when they are being overfed with minerals such as nitrogen. Cacti become thin and reluctant to produce flowers, while succulents produce spindly, lank, unattractive growth.

LIGHT

42 HOW MUCH LIGHT?

Most cacti and succulents need full sun during active periods of growth in order to stay healthy. They tolerate lower light levels in winter when they are dormant, but even then need a bright spot. When cultivating cacti and other succulents indoors, place plants directly in front of a window or in a conservatory. Natural daylight can be supplemented by artificial lights.

WHERE TO POSITION PLANTS IN A ROOM
Most desert cacti and succulents require bright natural light throughout the year. The area directly in front of a window is best; any place farther away is too dark.

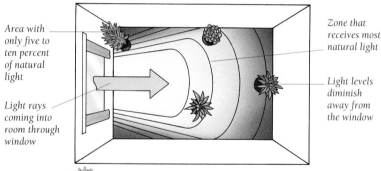

Area with only five to ten percent of natural light

Light rays coming into room through window

Zone that receives most natural light

Light levels diminish away from the window

43 THE EFFECTS OF POOR LIGHT

PALE SKIN DUE TO INADEQUATE LIGHT

Poor light and incorrect feeding of cacti and succulents produces one of two bad effects: either pale skin and elongated unhealthy growth, or stunted leaves on spindly shoots. To resume healthy growth, prune back affected stems and place the plant in bright light.

44 LIGHT-SENSITIVE PLANTS

A few cacti and some succulents are so light sensitive that they do not flower unless there are less than 12 hours of daylight. Even artificial light prevents flowering, so keep the plants in a little-used room until they bud.

Flowers open in winter

Flower color is affected by light

△ SCHLUMBERGERA 'FIRECRACKER'

Flowers open in late summer

◁ CRASSULA FALCATA

Fleshy silver-gray leaves

Glossy leaves dark green on top and deep red underneath

△ CRASSULA STREYI

45 PROVIDING LIGHT IN WINTER

Cacti and succulents tolerate less light in the winter months, when many are dormant, but even shade-loving *Epiphyllum* favor a bright spot. Place a mirror behind the plant to help provide even light, or buy artificial lights with wavelengths that have been adjusted to suit the plant's needs. These are sold at garden centers.

46 PLANTS TO GROW IN FULL SUN

Choose desert plants that thrive in dry conditions in full sun. These species are best cultivated outdoors in warmer climates with a minimum temperature of 61°F (16°C). Otherwise, they grow well in a sunny indoor site, such as on a windowsill or in a greenhouse.

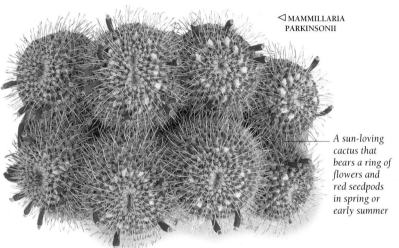

◁ MAMMILLARIA PARKINSONII

A sun-loving cactus that bears a ring of flowers and red seedpods in spring or early summer

---

PLANTS FOR FULL SUN
CACTI
Ariocarpus species
Astrophytum species
Cephalocereus species
Cleistocactus species
Echinopsis species
Mammillaria parkinsonii
SUCCULENTS
Agave utahensis
Aloe dichotoma
Conophytum species
Cyphostemma species
Gibbaeum species
Lampranthus species

This species from Mexico produces bright yellow flowers

◁ ASTROPHYTUM MYRIOSTIGMA

47 AVOID LEAF SCORCH

In summer, even plants that thrive on full sun can be susceptible to leaf scorch, especially if they are cultivated in a greenhouse. Hang blinds on the glass roof so that you can provide some protection, and when moving young plants out into full sun, cover in fabric until they have acclimatized.

△ ALOE
DICHOTOMA

Spiky leaves can be blue, gray, or deep green

Flowers open on summer nights

△ AGAVE
UTAHENSIS

Plant grows best in warmer climates

ECHINOPSIS ▷
MAMILLOSA
F. KERMESINA

35

48 PLANTS FOR DRY SHADE

These are predominantly desert plants that need dry conditions and diffuse rather than direct sun to flourish. Some of these plants are prone to rot if they become wet, and their leaves may scorch if exposed to the sun's rays for long periods.

Evergreen succulent with glossy green leaves

Leaves may be round or lance shaped

◁ CRASSULA OVATA

Orange-red bell-shaped flowers

Plant produces offsets to form a clump

Flower spikes are borne in late summer

△ x GRAPTOVERIA 'DEBBI'

PLANTS FOR DRY SHADE
CACTI
Echinopsis chamaecereus
  f. *lutea*
SUCCULENTS
Ceropegia woodii
Crassula ovata
Echeveria setosa
Euphorbia species
Gasteria species
Graptopetalum bellum
x *Graptoveria* 'Debbi'
Haworthia attenuata
Huernia species
Kalanchoe blossfeldiana

△ GRAPTOPETALUM
BELLUM

◁ ECHEVERIA
SETOSA

*Clumping plant
that rots in
damp conditions*

*Long red
thorns
similar to
cactus spines*

△ EUPHORBIA
HORRIDA

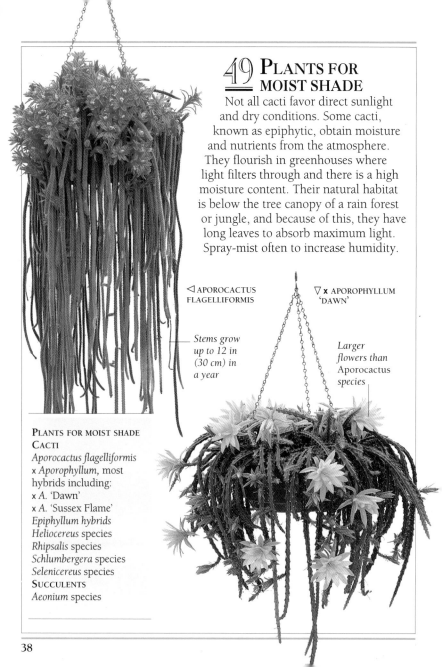

49 PLANTS FOR MOIST SHADE

Not all cacti favor direct sunlight and dry conditions. Some cacti, known as epiphytic, obtain moisture and nutrients from the atmosphere. They flourish in greenhouses where light filters through and there is a high moisture content. Their natural habitat is below the tree canopy of a rain forest or jungle, and because of this, they have long leaves to absorb maximum light. Spray-mist often to increase humidity.

◁ APOROCACTUS FLAGELLIFORMIS

Stems grow up to 12 in (30 cm) in a year

▽ x APOROPHYLLUM 'DAWN'

Larger flowers than Aporocactus species

PLANTS FOR MOIST SHADE
CACTI
Aporocactus flagelliformis
x *Aporophyllum,* most hybrids including:
x *A.* 'Dawn'
x *A.* 'Sussex Flame'
Epiphyllum hybrids
Heliocereus species
Rhipsalis species
Schlumbergera species
Selenicereus species
SUCCULENTS
Aeonium species

TEMPERATURE

50 TEMPERATURE FOR ACTIVE GROWTH

Most cacti species and some succulents grow in summer and are dormant in winter, but extremes of temperature – either hot or cold – can shock the plants into dormancy at any time of year. Most cacti and succulents need a temperature of 61°F (16°C) to grow, while tropical plants need higher temperatures of 70–90°F (21–32°C).

PLANTS GROWING IN A WINDOW
When mature, most cacti and succulents need full sun and warmth for growth. A sunny windowsill is the perfect site.

51 REVIVING COLD-DAMAGED PLANTS

A few cacti and succulents tolerate outdoor temperatures as low as 32°F (0°C) for very short periods but long periods of low temperatures can damage the soft, new growth of most plants and scar their tissue, and they will eventually collapse. To revive cold-damaged plants, increase the temperature to dry out dead tissue and prevent rot attack. If possible, cut out affected areas.

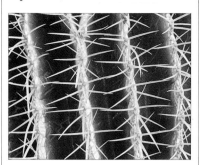

SCARRING ON STEM DUE TO COLD DAMAGE

52 DRAFT-FREE VENTILATION

In a greenhouse environment, provide draft-free ventilation in summer and winter for healthy plant growth. Ventilation reduces a buildup of moisture in the air, which can cause rot in many cacti. Plants grown in the house will also appreciate being moved outdoors into the fresh air in summer.

53 PROTECTION FROM FROST

Most cacti and succulents grow well outdoors only if the temperature does not fall below 41°F (5°C). To protect plants from occasional frosts in normally frost-free areas, wrap them in paper, plastic, or sacking. If cold damage occurs, it tends to attack only soft new growth, which can be cut out.

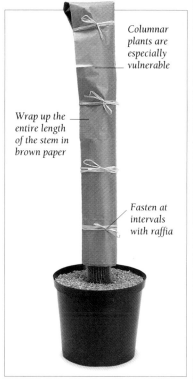

Columnar plants are especially vulnerable

Wrap up the entire length of the stem in brown paper

Fasten at intervals with raffia

PROTECTING TALL CACTI FROM FROST

54 PLANTS FOR WARM CLIMATES

These are cacti and succulents that are sensitive to cold climates and will flourish only if the temperature throughout the year does not fall below 61°F (16°C). In temperate regions, cultivate these plants indoors only, or in summer grow them outside in containers. Bring them inside before the cold weather arrives to avoid the danger of frost damage.

Rust red spines grow densely on unusual double crown

△ MELOCACTUS MATANZANUS

Spines fade with age

Dark glossy leaves with pale downy underside

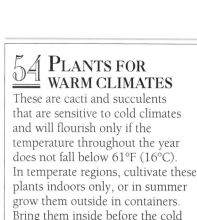

Flowers are produced from spring to fall

Leaves have prominent veins

ADENIUM ▷ OBESUM

Stem has toxic milky sap

PLANTS FOR WARM CLIMATES
CACTI
Echinocactus grusonii
Echinopsis chamaecereus f. *lutea*
Epiphyllum crenatum
Gymnocalycium mihanovichii
'Red Top'
Melocactus matanzanus
Rhipsalis crispata
SUCCULENTS
Adenium obesum
Brachystelma barberae
Caralluma species
Ceropegia woodii
Cyphostemma bainesii
Monadenium species
Pachypodium namaquanum
Sanseviera trifasciata

55 PLANTS FOR TEMPERATE CLIMATES

Although these cacti and succulents can withstand near-freezing outdoor temperatures for short periods before they suffer cold damage, they grow best when the temperature does not fall below 41°F (5°C). In areas where the winter temperature regularly falls below freezing, bring the plants indoors or place under cover.

Yellow-edged leaves grow up to 5 ft (1.5 m) long

AGAVE ▷
AMERICANA
'VARIEGATA'

Robust cactus with contorted blue-green stem

Often pot-grown so that it can be moved in out of the cold

◁ CEREUS
HILDMANNIANUS
VAR. MONSTROSE

PLANTS FOR TEMPERATE CLIMATES
CACTI
Aporocactus flagelliformis
Cereus hildmannianus
 var. *monstrosa*
Echinocereus, most species
 including:
E. cinerascens
SUCCULENTS
Aeonium arboreum
 'Atropurpureum'
Agave americana 'Variegata'
Echeveria elegans
Gasteria, most species
 including
G. batesiana
Gibbaeum album
Lampranthus haworthii
Lewisia cotyledon

Hybrid valued for its quill-like leaves

56 PLANTS FOR COLD CLIMATES

Some species of succulents are hardy and can survive winter temperatures as low as -30°F (-35°C), but only if they are kept dry or are protected by a layer of insulating snow. Most hardy succulents are low-growing or carpeting plants and make good all-year-round groundcover.

Swollen leaves protected by a downy layer

A hardy alpine well suited to rock gardens

Symmetrical rosette of pointed, scalelike leaves that turn from green to purple

SEMPERVIVUM △
'ODDITY'

PLANTS FOR COLD CLIMATES
SUCCULENTS
Sedum, many hardy species including:
S. acre
S. album
S. cauticolum
S. spectabile
S. spurium
Sempervivum
Most hybrids and species including:
S. arachnoideum
S. 'Emerson's Giant'
S. 'Oddity'

SEMPERVIVUM
'EMERSON'S GIANT' ▷

43

MAINTENANCE

57 CLEANING NON-HAIRY PLANTS

An indoor display will last for two or three years before it needs replanting, and in that time dust will collect on the leaf surface. To keep the smooth, shiny leaves common to many succulents looking healthy, gently dust them from time to time with a soft artist's brush. For best results, dust carefully between any small gaps.

DUSTING LEAVES WITH A PAINT BRUSH

58 DUSTING SPINY PLANTS

Many cacti are grown indoors on sunny windowsills and, like any decorative object, they soon start to gather dust. In addition to looking unsightly, a thick layer of dust may prevent the plant from converting sunlight into chlorophyll during photosynthesis and, in time, this may impede growth. Use a hair dryer to remove dust from spiny plants; it is effective and your hands are protected. Set the hair dryer to a slow, cool setting and, holding the hair dryer about 6 in (15 cm) from the spines of the plant, gently blow away the dust.

Don't hold dryer too close to plant

Particles of dust gather on narrow spines

BLOWING AWAY DUST PARTICLES

59 DEADHEADING

After flowering, deadheading is necessary to maintain both the appearance and health of the plant. The easiest way to deadhead is with your fingers. Grip the flower between your thumb and forefinger and carefully pinch it off. This process may have to be repeated several times during the flowering season.

PINCHING OFF DEAD FLOWERHEADS

PLUCKING OFF A DAMAGED LEAF

60 REMOVING DEAD LEAVES OR SHOOTS

Dead or damaged leaves or shoots may harbor pests and diseases. Good hygiene involves removing these dead or damaged areas to keep the plant in good condition. With rosette-shaped succulents, grip the leaf at its base close to the stem and pull it off cleanly. Pinch out shoots above a healthy joint.

61 CUTTING OUT DAMAGED AREAS

Cacti and succulents can become damaged if their cultural needs are not met. The leaves and stems of succulents growing close to the roots turn brown and may have to be removed if the rest of the plant is to survive. Using pruners, cut out the problem stems. When all the damaged matter has been dealt with, feed and water correctly.

TRIMMING WITH PRUNERS

62 WHY PRUNE?

Most succulents and some leafy cacti need pruning to keep their shape and to produce new shoots. Pruning removes straggly growth that impairs the plant's vigor and makes it less open to attack by pests. Prune shrubby succulents in spring, winter-flowering succulents in summer, and leafy epiphytic cacti after flowering. If pruned often, plants become woody and need replacing.

63 HOW TO PRUNE

Always use a sharp pair of pruners when pruning. Blunt pruning tools create ragged cuts that may become infected. Trim shrubby plants to just above a shoot or bud. To improve the look of mounding or creeping plants, remove old brown foliage from beneath new growth. For trailing plants, cut back long stems to encourage bushy growth near the stem base. Frequently pruned succulents may become woody.

STRAGGLY GROWTH NEEDS PRUNING

1 Select top-heavy leaves that have branched out from the parent stem. Using sharp anvil pruners, cut straight across the stem just below the leaf joint. To prevent disease, cut as close as you can to the joint and do not leave a stub.

2 Using clean, straight cuts, prune out old, stunted, or diseased stems that are situated at the base of the plant and unlikely to produce a crop of flowers.

3 To prevent the death of shoot tips (dieback), remove any brown stem ends. Cut across the healthy section of the stem just below the brown tip.

4 To encourage new flowering shoots, prune back old stems that have already flowered until they are level with young shoots. Make an angled cut across the vein of the old leaf, at a point just above where the new shoot begins.

PRUNED INTO SHAPE

64 WHY REPOT?

All cacti and succulents need repotting from time to time for the following reasons: to allow enough room for maximum root growth – cramped roots cannot absorb nutrients and growth is inhibited; to loosen compacted soil so that air and water can circulate; and to correct the mineral imbalance caused by long-term watering.

Brown leaf tips indicate poor plant health

PLANT IN NEED OF REPOTTING ▷
Roots growing out through the base of the pot are a sure sign that this fast-growing succulent needs repotting.

Large, full-depth pot allows for new growth

65 TEASING OUT POT-BOUND ROOTS

Take the plant out of its container and examine its roots for disease. Handle with care since plants that have not been repotted for years, or those kept in too wet or too dry conditions, often have fragile root systems. If the rootball has become compacted and you intend to plant it in the same type of soil mix as in the original pot, gently break up the rootball to help the roots grow. If using a different soil mix, first shake off most of the old soil.

Be careful with the feeding roots

◁ LOOSENING A COMPACTED ROOTBALL
Prepare the plant for repotting by teasing out compacted roots. Examine the roots and cut out any that are old or damaged.

66 HOW TO REPOT A CACTUS

The best time to repot cacti and succulents is at the start of the growing season. Choose a clean pot that is large enough to accommodate new growth. Plants smaller than 6 in (15 cm) are best grown in half pots 1 in (2.5 cm) wider than the plant's diameter; taller plants need full-depth pots 2–4 in (5–10 cm) wider than the plant's diameter.

1 Scrub the pot with soapy water so that it is germ-free. Place a little soil mix in the base and use another pot to mark the size of the plant's roots.

2 Fill in between the two pots with soil mix to within ½ in (1 cm) of the rims. Press down on the inner pot to firm the soil mix and to leave a hole.

3 Lay the plant on its side and twist off the old pot. Remove any old loose soil mix from the rootball and tease out the roots. Cut out any dead roots.

4 Holding the plant at the top of the rootball, carefully drop it into the hole. Straighten it and lightly firm the soil mix. Sprinkle with topdressing.

PROPAGATION

67 WHY PROPAGATE?

Propagation is a low-cost way of obtaining new cacti and succulent plants, and it is the only way to increase the presence of rare and endangered species. There are several methods: taking cuttings or dividing a plant to reproduce hybrids; raising from seed, which yields new plant types; and grafting, which suits more difficult species.

CLEARLY LABEL
YOUNG PLANTS

68 RAISING FROM SEED

For best results, grow plants from fresh seed rather than old commercial seed. Collect the seed from the plants after the seedpods have ripened. Squash the wet seed onto a paper towel and let dry. When dry, put the seed through a strainer to remove any chaff.

1 Fill a pot to the brim with cactus potting mix and firm. Scatter the seed over the soil mix. Stand the pot in tepid water. Let drain, then topdress.

2 Label the pot and cover in a plastic bag. Leave in bright shade with a minimum temperature of 66°F (19°C), or 70–81°F (21–27°C) for faster results.

69 SOWING LARGE SEEDS

Small seeds can be sprinkled over the soil surface but larger seeds need to be pressed down into the soil mix until they sit at twice their own depth. Allow at least ½ in (1 cm) between seeds so that they have room to develop. Some of the larger seeds have a thick outer coating. Before sowing, put these seeds in a refrigerator for 48 hours.

PLANTING LARGE SEEDS

70 PRICKING OUT SEEDLINGS

When the seeds germinate in about 2–4 weeks, remove the plastic bag to improve ventilation. Grow them on at a minimum temperature of 50°F (10°C) in a bright location but out of direct sunlight, which may scorch young plants. When the seedlings are big enough to be handled without damaging their roots (several months to a year, depending on the species), prick them out. Plant seedlings less than 1 in (2.5 cm) in trays and larger ones in pots.

1 Prick out seedlings when they begin to crowd one another. With a spoon, carefully ease small clumps with their soil mix out of the pot.

2 Taking care not to damage the delicate roots, separate each seedling from the clump, saving as much soil mix as possible with the roots.

3 Almost fill several 2 in (5 cm) pots with cactus potting mix. Plant each seedling in a pot and dress with gravel. Water 3–4 days later.

71 CROSS-POLLINATION

For plants to produce seed, pollen must be carried from the flowers of one plant to another. Outdoors this is achieved naturally, but indoor plants need cross-pollinating by hand. First isolate the flower to protect it from other plants' pollen.

Stigma

Stamen

Anther

1 ▷ When ripe and laden with pollen, gently dab the anthers with a fine artist's brush to pick up pollen.

2 △ Carefully brush the pollen onto the stigma of a flower on another plant of the same species. When seeds form, collect and label them with their parentage details.

72 TAKING LEAF CUTTINGS

A quick and simple method of propagating succulents, such as *Gasteria* and some *Haworthia*, is to take leaf cuttings. Take the cuttings when the plant starts active growth, and they will root in 3–12 weeks.

1 Holding the plant steady, select a young healthy leaf and pull it away from the stem. Place the leaf to dry in a warm, dry site for a day or two, or until a callus has formed over the wound.

2 Fill a small pot with cactus potting soil mix to within 2 in (5 cm) of the rim. Set the leaf in the soil and cover the surface in gravel. Keep the pot just damp, in partial shade at 64°F (18°C).

73 TAKING STEM CUTTINGS

Many succulents, except those that have water-storing tissue in a swollen rootstock, are propagated in this way. Take stem cuttings in spring when a plant starts active growth, and avoid long cuttings, which wilt before they take root.

2 △ Trim the cut stem so that it is only 2–4 in (5–10 cm) long. Remove any leaves from the base. Place the stem in a warm site until a callus forms on the cut.

1 △ Choose a healthy sturdy stem. Steady the plant and slice the stem with a small sharp knife just above a bud or a new shoot. Do not leave a stub.

3 △ Plant the cutting in a small pot one third full of cactus potting mix and the rest gravel. Keep just moist in an airy, bright site for between 2–6 weeks.

74 HOW TO STOP BLEEDING STEMS

When cut or wounded, all *Euphorbia* and some succulents in the family *Asclepiadaceae* produce a milky white sap. To stop the flow of stems that bleed, dip the cut end in tepid water for a few seconds. Avoid getting sap on your skin since it can cause irritation. If the parent plant is bleeding, hold a damp cloth against the wound.

75 TAKING STEM SECTIONS

Plants that have flattened, leaflike stems, such as *Epiphyllum*, and many columnar cacti, can be propagated from a section of stem rather than a complete stem. The section should be taken at the end of the dormant period and usually takes 3–12 weeks to root.

1 Using a clean, sharp knife, cut a stem into 9 in (23 cm) sections. Place in a warm, dry place to form calluses.

2 Fill a small pot one-third full of cactus potting mix and the rest gravel. Insert the end of the stem.

76 DIVISION OF CLUMP-FORMING OFFSETS

Some cacti, for example, *Mammillaria* and *Echinopsis*, and succulents, such as *Haworthia* and *Gasteria*, grow to form a clump of leaves with many offsets. Those offsets, which develop roots, can be divided off from the parent plant in spring, and grown on as new plants.

1 Using a widger or spoon, dig out and pull away larger offsets from the parent plant. Dust the stem wound with fungicide and leave the offset to callus.

2 Fill a small pot with soil mix and insert the offset to the same depth as it sat in the parent pot. Topdress with gravel and place in sun or bright shade.

77 DIVISION OF OFFSET TUBERS

Succulents with tuberous roots, such as *Senecio* and *Ceropegia* form other tubers, offset from the parent plant, just below soil level.

To obtain new plants, divide up these offsets and grow them on. Water sparingly until the roots are established to avoid rot.

1 Dig into the soil mix with a widger or spoon to locate an offset tuber. Sever it from the main tuber and lift out.

2 Leave the tuber to callus. If it has roots, plant it in cactus potting mix. If not, use gravel with only a little mix.

78 DIVISION OF ROOTSTOCKS

This method of division is used for species that have swollen rootstocks with several growing points. Division is undertaken

when the plant is dormant. This propagation method is also used to retain variegated color on plants grown from cultivars of *Sanseviera*.

1 Dig up the parent plant (*Sanseviera trifasciata*), or remove it from its pot. Cut the rootstock into sections, making sure each one has its own growing point.

2 Cut away any part of the rootstock that is damaged. Dust the cuts with fungicide and let callus. Replant each section in cactus potting mix.

79 SPLIT-GRAFTING

A technique for propagating difficult and slow-growing cacti whereby the top growth of the plant is grafted onto the rootstock of a more vigorous species. When grafted, the growth rate can be increased tenfold. Leafy cacti, such as *Schlumbergera,* respond well to split-grafting if propagated at the start of the spring growing season.

1 Cleanly slice off the top 1 in (2.5 cm) of a vigorous rootstock to form a base on which a plant can be grafted.

2 Make a vertical incision (½–¾ in) 1–2 cm deep, passing through the central core tissue of the rootstock.

3 Select a healthy stem for grafting (1–2 leaf sections long if it is a *Schlumbergera*). Cut it across the joint of the leaf.

4 Trim away the lower ½ in (1 cm). Slice away the skin from both sides until it tapers to fit into the split in the stock.

5 Wedge the prepared cutting (scion) into the split in the rootstock. Ensure that both central core tissues make contact.

6 Push a spine through both pieces to hold the scion in place, and bind with raffia. Leave to grow in a bright, airy site.

80 FLAT-GRAFTING

This method of grafting is used to propagate most types of cacti with contorted growth habits and those whose seedlings may lack chlorophyll. Choose a healthy cactus for a rootstock; *Echinopsis* species work well. When preparing the graft, make sure that your hands are clean, since cut surfaces can be infected by fungal diseases.

1 Using a clean knife, slice to a depth of 1 in (2.5 cm) below the crown of the stock, to expose the core tissue.

2 Remove about ¼ in (6 mm) of skin from around the edges of the stock to ensure both core tissues will make contact.

3 Cut off the scion and bevel away ¼ in (6 mm) of skin from around the edges to reveal the core tissue.

4 Place the cut surfaces of the scion and stock together and rotate the scion to remove any air pockets. Fasten together with rubber bands and within two weeks the graft will start to grow.

START OF NEW GROWTH

MAMILLARIA HERRERAE

PESTS & DISEASES

81 IDENTIFYING FUNGAL DISEASES

Although cacti and other succulents are not prone to disease, dampness and poor ventilation produces the conditions in which fungal spores thrive, as does the failure to remove damaged leaves or stems. Most fungal infections occur during late spring or fall. On these cold nights, condensation collects on the leaves of plants cultivated indoors and out and fails to evaporate by morning. Fungal spores develop in beads of water and soon attack the plant tissue.

FUNGAL LEAF SPOT
Brown spots appear and, if not dealt with, result in leaf drop. Burn infected leaves and treat the plant with copper sulfate.

CORKY SCAB
Corklike spots develop near the stem base due to disease damage in the past or poor cultivation. Improve growing conditions.

82 PREVENTATIVE MEASURES

If cultivated in the right environment and properly cared for, cacti and succulents should stay healthy. Inspect plants from time to time so that any signs of poor health can be remedied. Carefully check new plants for pests and diseases to avoid their spread.

83 COMMON PESTS

Pests are a common problem that can be controlled by chemical pesticides or, when plants are cultivated in a greenhouse, by introducing a natural predator. Systemic pesticides are successful because they are absorbed into the plant sap, poisoning any insect that feeds on the plant. During the growing season, use a systemic pesticide 2–3 times as a simple preventative measure. Water the solution onto the plant's roots, not its stem; its waxy skin will just repel any moisture. If an infestation appears, use weekly for 3–4 weeks.

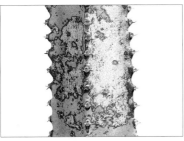

SPIDER MITE DAMAGE
This mite thrives in dry, hot greenhouses, attacking young growth. Increase the humidity or use a predator mite to kill it.

SCALE INSECTS
Attacks stems and lower leaves. Plant growth is checked and sooty mold quickly appears. Treat with a systemic pesticide.

MEALY BUGS
White nests and a sticky honeydew cover infested plants. Treat with a systemic insecticide or, in temperatures above 70°F (21°C), introduce a predator ladybug.

SLUGS & SNAILS
Holes in leaves and slimy trails are signs of slug or snail infestation. Epiphytes that favor damp, shady places are vulnerable, so scatter slug pellets between the plants.

FAVORITE CACTI

84 x APOROPHYLLUM

Ideal plants for hanging baskets, this collection of hybrids is distinguished by its large, open-faced flowers in brilliant shades of orange, cerise, scarlet, purple, and also white. The slender stems grow over 6 ft (2 m) long. Simple to grow, the plants need a fairly rich soil mix, shade, and temperatures no lower than 43°F (6°C). They flower best if fed during spring and summer.

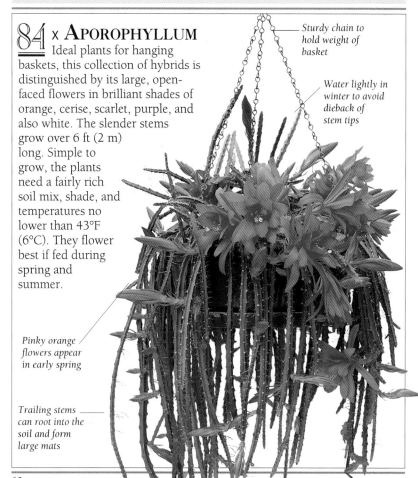

Sturdy chain to hold weight of basket

Water lightly in winter to avoid dieback of stem tips

Pinky orange flowers appear in early spring

Trailing stems can root into the soil and form large mats

85 ECHINOCEREUS KNIPPELIANUS

Clump of mature slow-growing stems

A striking cactus that produces pink flowers and green berries near the stem tips in spring. The swollen, dark green stems are slow growing, reaching a spread of 15 in (38 cm). It grows best in temperatures no lower than 41°F (5°C) and prefers bright shade to sun; in the wild, the roots pull the plant below ground to avoid hot sun.

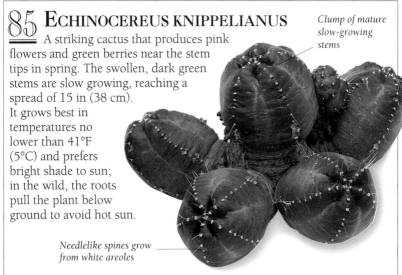

Needlelike spines grow from white areoles

86 ECHINOPSIS 'FORTY-NINER'

Spiny necks can be 10 in (25 cm) long

Like other *Echinopsis* hybrids, this sun loving, globular cactus was bred to produce a large plant with vivid yellow flowers. The blooms are night flowering and open at dusk. The flowers fade within 24 hours, but produce several flushes of flowers throughout spring and summer. This cactus is incredibly robust and can withstand neglect and near-freezing temperatures as low as 36°F (2°C).

Vivid yellow flowers open at dusk

87 GYMNOCALYCIUM HORSTII

Flowers only open fully in bright light

A small globular cactus, that flowers freely when young from late spring to the end of summer. Waxy, plum-shaped, green fruits appear soon after. Position this cactus in bright shade rather than full sun, which may scorch the plant's skin and stunt its growth, and protect it from winter cold and frost.

88 MAMMILLARIA HAHNIANA

This sun-loving cactus flowers prolifically, even when young, making it a good species to have in a collection. It is commonly known as the "birthday cake cactus," because after it has flowered in spring, red seedpods appear and stand in a ring on the crown like candles on a cake.

89 MATUCANA INTERTEXTA

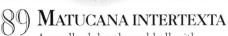

A small, globe-shaped ball with brown needlelike spines, this cactus produces bright red or orange flowers with long necks. The cactus does not flower until the plant is 3–5 years old, and then the blooms appear in spring or summer, or sometimes in both seasons. *Matucana* species grow well in sunny sites, with a minimum temperature of 50°F (10°C) to avoid cold damage and root rot. When mature, the plant may develop into a clump.

90 NEOPORTERIA CLAVATA

This is another sun-loving, globular cactus that flowers freely – once the plant has reached a diameter of 2–3 in (5–8 cm) – in spring and then again in fall. Keep this cactus at a temperature above 50°F (10°C). Lightly water it at intervals during the dormant winter period to prevent the roots from drying out and to guard against scarring.

△ SIDE VIEW

Pink flowers set against dark spines

VIEW FROM
ABOVE ▷

91 PARODIA CONCINNA

Originally from South America, this species, like most other *Parodia*, enjoys sun and a light spray-misting on mild winter days to prevent the roots from drying out. Be careful not to water when it is very cold as the roots may rot. Flowers appear in spring and summer, and are golden yellow with maroon stigmas. Soft spines cover the plant body and vary in color from yellow to red. With age, the plant produces offsets and forms a clump.

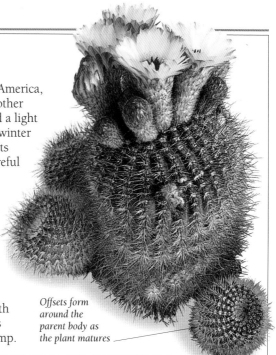

Offsets form around the parent body as the plant matures

92 STENOCACTUS MULTICOSTATUS

The beauty of this cactus lies in the delicate pink flowers with darker pink stripes that grow from the plant crown in spring and summer. These blooms are set against a mass of copper-brown spines. *Stenocactus* species are sun-loving and cannot withstand temperatures lower than 41°F (5°C). Position them where they can be viewed from above to enjoy their spectacular floral display.

FAVORITE SUCCULENTS

93 AEONIUM ARBOREUM 'SCHWARTZKOPF'

This fast-growing, rosette-shaped succulent with dark purple leaves makes a good feature plant for summer borders. It is fairly robust and can withstand chilly conditions, although dampness causes rot. If planted in a bright site, it retains its color through winter.

Growing point at center of mature rosette

94 AGAVE VICTORIA-REGINAE

This robust succulent is fairly commonplace; it enjoyed an early popularity in cultivation. Although slow growing, it produces an attractive domed rosette of dark green leaves, each tipped with a spine and edged and patterned in white. Small flowers appear after 20–30 years when the plant reaches a diameter of 2–3 ft (60–90 cm). Although sun-loving, it can tolerate temperatures as low as 36°F (2°C).

95 ALOE PLICATILIS

Narrow blue-green leaves form a fan shape

A sun-loving succulent that grows to form a large bush or tree with a spread of 10 ft (3 m). Although dormant over summer, this species flowers annually from late spring and into summer with sparse red or orange-red blooms.

Grows to become a large bush or tree

96 CRASSULA ARBORESCENS

This is a commonly cultivated fleshy-leaved succulent that matures into a bush 10 ft (3 m) high with a 4 ft (1.2 m) spread. The blue-green leaves of this large species are thick and waxy and, if grown in sun, the leaf edges have red margins.

Prune this *Crassula* regularly to prevent the leaves from weighing down the stem. Long-lasting pink flowers appear in the fall, providing winter color.

97 DUDLEYA BRITTONII

A flowerlike succulent with a relatively slow-growing small rosette of silver white leaves, this cactus has a pronounced silvery bloom. Keep the plant leaves dry during cold weather. The minimum temperature it can tolerate is 50°F (10 °C). In summer, masses of small, pale yellow flowers are borne on 3 ft (90 cm) stems.

98 ECHEVERIA TUNDELLII

This attractive and easy-to-grow species produces offsets of soft blue rosettes that develop into a small mound. The rosettes begin to flower when they are only 1 in (2.5 cm) in diameter, and produce brilliant flame-red flowers.

Generally sun-loving, *Echeveria* are more intensely colored when grown outdoors, but they make good houseplants for a bright site.

Arching stems carry red and yellow flowers

Small rosettes of leaves grow into a mound

99 HAWORTHIA COARCTATA VAR. ADELAIDENSIS

Haworthia are predominantly rosette-shaped species, but this is one of the few plants in the genus to form clumps of tough leafy columns. Its interest lies in its ability to change color: in cooler weather when it starts to grow, the leaves are dark green, but when dormant in hot sun, they turn a rich purple-red. This species prefers diffuse sun and will offset freely.

△ SIDE VIEW

Tightly packed scalelike leaves curve in toward the stem tip

△ VIEW FROM ABOVE

*Leaf heads form
a small clump
above the
soil surface*

100 LITHOPS SALICOLA

A tiny succulent with swollen leaves the size of pebbles, this *Lithops* is one of the taller species, and its slate gray leaf heads stand above the soil surface. In hot weather, it becomes semidormant, and then in early fall, white daisylike flowers grow. This succulent will not tolerate poor light or incorrect watering.

*Daisylike flowers
grow out of the
fissure between a
pair of leaves*

101 SEMPERVIVUM ARACHNOIDEUM

A small, hardy alpine, this succulent is common in the wild and in cultivation, and makes a suitable subject for a rock garden. Its neat rosette of leaves offsets freely in spring to form a spreading carpet of foliage. In summer, the rosettes of this species are covered in a "cobweb" of filaments.

INDEX

Acknowledgments

Dorling Kindersley would like to thank Hilary Bird for compiling the index, Lesley Malkin for proofreading, and Robert Campbell for page makeup assistance.

Photography
KEY: t *top*; b *bottom*; c *center*; l *left*; r *right*
All photographs by Peter Anderson and Steve Gorton except for:
Linda Burgess 39; Geoff Dann 8, 9cr; Jeff Foot 10b; John Glover 19tr; Dave King 14, 15cl, 16, 17cl, 17bl, 18, 20tr, 21tl, 21b, 22, 28br; Jorge Provenza 10tr; Juliette Wade 2; Matthew Ward 15br, 25br, 26b, 27tl, 29, 31, 40br, 44bl, 45tr, 45br, 52b.

Illustrations
Andrew Farmer